Stupid California

Other Books by Leland Gregory

Stupid California

Leland Gregory

Andrews McMeel
Publishing, LLC

Kansas City • Sydney • London

10 11 12 13 14 RR2 10 9 8 7 6 5 4 3 2 1

ISBN-13: 978-0-7407-9134-5
ISBN-10: 0-7407-9134-6

Library of Congress Control Number: 2009940821

www.andrewsmcmeel.com

Attention: Schools and Businesses

Andrews McMeel books are available at quantity discounts with bulk purchase for
educational, business, or sales promotional use. For information, please write to: Special
Sales Department, Andrews McMeel Publishing, LLC, 1130 Walnut Street, Kansas City,
Missouri 64106.

Stupid
California

A Deadbeat Tenant

In early 1996, a California judge ruled against James Pflugradt's estate and in favor of his former landlord. The judge said the landlord could keep Pflugradt's $825 security deposit because Pflugradt died without giving thirty days' notice.

The post office sent postcards to local residents informing them that the Pleasanton branch had extended its hours during the 2005 Christmas rush (December 6–December 21)—but didn't deliver the cards until December 21.

What's the Rush?

"The whole country from San Francisco to Los Angeles, and from the sea shore to the base of the Sierra Nevadas, resounds with the sordid cry of gold, GOLD, GOLD! while the field is left half-planted, the house half-built, and everything neglected but the manufacture of shovels and pickaxes."

The Californian, May 29, 1848

The newspaper also announced it was suspending publication because of staff leaving to seek their fortunes during the gold rush. It ceased publication completely on June 14, 1848.

The Blind Leading the Blind

Even though George Edgar Lizarralde was legally blind, the Department of Motor Vehicles in Santa Ana issued him a driver's license in 1985. Lizarralde had failed the test three times, and even though he again failed the vision test on the fourth try, he was granted the license. During his January 1994 trial for mowing down Deborah Ann Mohr in a crosswalk while she crossed the street, the DMV's negligence was judged the main cause of the 1990 accident.

"25 Women Arrived on Different Vessels Today."

Alta California newspaper, December 20, 1849

Earth to Mr. Davis, Earth to Mr. Davis

"My vision is to make the most diverse state on earth, and we have people from every planet on the earth in this state. We have the sons and daughters of every—of people from every planet, of every country on earth . . ."

Former Governor Gray Davis,
hoping to avoid a recall vote, September 17, 2003

Hot Car, Cold Fish

Twenty-year-old Jonathan Fish had finished smoking a cigarette as he drove across the San Francisco Bay Bridge and flicked the still lit cigarette out the window. But the wind blew the cigarette into the backseat of his $30,000 white Ford Expedition SUV, setting it on fire. He jumped out of the car without putting it into park, and watched helplessly as it started to roll, crashing into a guardrail by the exit and burning to the frame. According to a February 18, 2005, article in the *San Francisco Chronicle,* Fish was cited by the California Highway Patrol for littering.

Amador, California, named after Jose Maria Amador, is the only county in the state named after a native Californian.

A Lame New Law

The Disabled Services Office of Valley College in Los Angeles set a new campus speed limit of 4 mph, with penalties for violators ranging from a simple warning to expulsion. So was the new policy to stop skateboarders from half-piping into other students? Nope. According to a December 14, 2002, article in the *Los Angeles Times,* it was enacted for students in wheelchairs. So, has there been a rash of accidents between students in wheelchairs and pedestrians? Nope. "It's a safety issue," said Vice President of Administration Tom Jacobsmeyer. "A speeding wheelchair can be just as dangerous as a speeding car."

Sax and Violins

Missourians who settled and mined in an area six miles east of Plymouth in Amador County in 1849 named their town Fiddletown (because when they couldn't mine they fiddled around). But one prominent citizen, Judge Columbus Allen Purinton (who was never a judge in Amador County), didn't like being referred to as "the man from Fiddletown" during his trips to San Francisco. Purinton got a bill passed through the state legislature on May 24, 1878, officially changing the town's name to Oleta, after his daughter. After the judge died, local citizens were tired of fiddling around with the town's name and had it changed back to Fiddletown on July 1, 1932.

Rubber Baby Buggy Bumpers

Apparently a seventeen-year-old girl was startled when she heard a cry from her baby, lost control of her car, and crashed on a freeway near Pleasanton. The girl was unharmed but was charged with driving without a license and the baby was eventually deactivated. The "baby" was an educational doll given to her in school, according to a December 2006 article in the *Contra Costa Times,* and programmed to cry when it needed to be fed, changed, or comforted. "When officers arrived, she was still caring for the baby," said a California Highway Patrol spokesman.

In August 2000, seven people at a
nudist convention in Jacumba
were treated with severe burns to
their feet after performing a
fire-walking ceremony.

We'll Leave
the Light On for You

Measure G, or the Transient Occupancy Tax, was placed
on the ballot in Cotati for the November 7, 2006, election.
The measure simply proposed raising the hotel tax in town
from 10 percent to 12 percent. No big deal, right? The
problem, according to Fred H. Levin, executive director
of the Sonoma County Taxpayers' Association, is, "There
are no hotels, motels, inns, or lodges in Cotati." Not to be
thwarted for such a silly little fact, Councilwoman Lisa
Moore rebutted, "We're being proactive." The measure
didn't measure up logically to the town members and was
defeated at the polls. This is kind of a perversion of *Field of
Dreams*—if you build it, they will tax it.

Harboring a Misunderstanding

On October 19, 1842, Commodore Thomas Catesby Jones of the U.S. Pacific Fleet, believing that Mexico had declared war on the United States, sailed into Monterey Harbor and demanded that the governor surrender California to the United States. Surrender documents were signed and on October 21, Jones went ashore to claim the land and raise the American flag. While speaking with prominent residents and glancing through the local paper, he realized that Mexico *hadn't* declared war on the United States—he quickly removed the American flag, replaced it with the Mexican one, removed his occupation forces, and sailed away in embarrassment.

California's state animal is the California grizzly bear, which is also on the state flag. The bear was honored in 1953, a full thirty-one years after the last known bear was killed.

You Better Hide Your Nuts

City officials in Santa Monica announced a really squirrelly plan in 2005 that made it unnecessary for male squirrels to hide their nuts anymore. The city administered birth control shots to the city's squirrels using GonaCon, a serum that halts ovulation in female squirrels and testicular development in males. The makers of the drug say the shot, which costs $2 to $10 per dose, does not have any dangerous side effects—but apparently no one asked the squirrels about that.

Open Mouth—
Insert Foot

"She's either Puerto Rican, or the same thing as Cuban, I mean they are all very hot. They have the, you know, part of the black blood in them and part of the Latino blood in them that together makes it."

Governor Arnold Schwarzenegger, on California's only
Latina Republican, Assemblywoman Bonnie Garcia, March 3, 2006

"SHOES ARE REQUIRED TO EAT IN ANY RESTAURANT OR OTHER PLACE SERVING FOOD TO THE PUBLIC."

• • • •

Strangely phrased law from Redding

The Political Circus

In October 2006, Kenneth Kahn announced he was running for mayor of Alameda, and he wasn't just clowning around. Kahn, who is known professionally as "Kenny the Clown," admitted he was a long shot, not because he's a clown (almost a prerequisite these days) but because he'd never run for elected office before. "People ask me, 'Do we really want to elect a clown for mayor of the city?'" Kahn said. "I say, 'That's an excellent question.'" The answer to that question, however, was ultimately no. Kahn got only 7 percent of the vote, losing out to Beverly Johnson. It's probably a good thing that Kahn didn't become mayor, because the person who would have eventually succeeded him would have had some pretty big shoes to fill.

Getting a Snout Full

A law passed on January 24, 1847, stated that all stray hogs in Yerba Buena must be securely penned or the hogs will be confiscated and the owner fined $5. Six days later Yerba Buena changed its name to San Francisco.

I'll Gopher That

Two janitors at a Ceres school were hospitalized and sixteen pupils injured in a failed attempt by the janitors to kill a gopher. After catching the gopher the two janitors decided the best way to kill him would be by pouring a gum- and wax-removing compound on him, which they did. After the ordeal, one of the janitors needed a break and lit a cigarette. Bad move. The gopher exploded, injuring the janitors, the students, and, of course, the gopher.

The City of Los Angeles announced
a major overhaul of its jury system
in 1995. Included in the $4 million
restructuring was the issuance of
mandatory thank-you notes to jurors.

Letting the Cat Out of the Bag

A woman in Antioch walked into a local police station and asked if officers could run a test on some merchandise she thought might have been tampered with. Much to the surprise of the officer on duty, the woman produced a bag filled with methamphetamines. She was concerned her boyfriend might have mixed in some hallucinogens. The next trip the woman took wasn't drug induced—it was police induced.

"Those who survived the San Francisco earthquake said, 'Thank God, I'm still alive.' But, of course, those who died, their lives will never be the same again."

Senator Barbara Boxer, Democrat

I Need That Like I Need a Hole in the Head

An August 2000 workplace brawl in Irvine quickly turned fatal when one man grabbed another in a headlock and put a gun to his head. The man reportedly fired the gun, shooting his victim in the face–but the victim wasn't the one who died. The bullet passed through the man's cheek and lodged deep in the shooter's own chest–killing him. This guy went from giving a headlock to getting a headstone.

"Speed upon country roads will be limited to ten miles an hour unless the motorist sees a bailiff who does not appear to have had a drink in thirty days, then the driver will be permitted to make what he can."

El Dorado County law

Urine Trouble Now

The *San Diego Union-Tribune* reported on September 22, 2000, that about a hundred employees became dizzy and nauseous at the National Pen Corporation's offices in Rancho Bernardo. Twenty-four employees were taken to the hospital while crews in hazardous-materials suits swept through the offices looking for the cause of the outbreak. It was determined that the culprit was an excessive number of urinal cakes in the third-floor men's bathroom.

Hang Five

In June 2000, a young man walking along the railroad tracks in San Clemente suffered a broken arm when a passing train knocked the surfboard out of his hands.

The Eagle Theatre, California's first theater, opened on Front Street in Sacramento on October 18, 1849. On January 8, 1850, less than three months later, it was washed away during the Great Flood (also called the Great Inundation) of 1850.

Time in a Bottle

A number of residents of Livermore, including people who worked for two nuclear labs in the area, were forced to dig randomly in July 1999 to look for a time capsule that had been buried twenty-five years earlier. The capsule, about the size of a beer keg, was heralded with great fanfare in 1974 but buried clandestinely by a work crew to deter thieves. The time capsule has yet to be unearthed.

Livermore is also home to the Livermore Centennial Light, which according to the *Guinness Book of World Records* has been burning continuously since 1901.

What's Bugging You, Man?

Radio station KVML-AM in Sonora reported on June 1, 2007, about Jamestown resident Mike Harstad, who attempted to destroy a wasp's nest with a can of Pledge and a cigarette lighter. The flame created by igniting the spray from the can got out of control and ultimately burned down his mobile home—the fire also destroyed an outbuilding, a truck, and a boat and trailer.

During the 1980s, in a bold stroke against terrorism, the Chico City Council banned nuclear weapons, enacting a mandatory $500 fine for anyone detonating a nuclear weapon within city limits. The question is, who would be around to collect?

Don't Point That at Me—I Might Go Off!

Police were called to investigate an armed robbery at the Mustang Books adult bookstore in Upland and found themselves in a three-hour car chase with the suspect, who had commandeered a taxicab. After two minor collisions the suspected robber, Steven McDermott, jumped out of the cab and hightailed it on foot, according to a November 3, 2007, report in the *Inland Valley Daily Bulletin*. Police surrounded McDermott, and when he reached toward his waistband, one officer shot and wounded him. It was soon discovered that McDermott wasn't reaching for a gun but for a phallic sex toy, which police said he did not steal from the bookstore. "Evidently, he had it tethered to his belt loop for whatever reason," a police spokesman said.

Can't See the Forest for the Trees

On a beautiful, sunny July day in 2001, Mark Vargas chatted with his neighbors, Richard Treanor and Carolynn Bissett, and told them he planned to install solar panels on his house. It sounded great to the staunch environmentalists and Prius-driving couple until Vargas told them they would have to cut down some of their large redwood trees because the shade would obstruct the panels. And according to the 1978 Solar Shade Control Act, Vargas had every right to make the request. After seven years of protests and court battles, according to a January 24, 2008, article in the *San Jose Mercury News,* a judge ordered two of the eight redwoods cut down.

More turkeys are raised in California than in any other state in the United States.

I Won't Tolerate Intolerance

According to a November 15, 2007, article in the *Chicago Sun-Times,* seventy people in a West Hollywood neighborhood petitioned the courts to disallow a local museum from, among other things, expanding its structure and extending its hours of operation until midnight. The angry neighbors were fed up with the intolerance they felt they were being subjected to by–the Museum of Tolerance.

It's Not Polite to Point

We all know the scene in the movies where the would-be robber sticks his finger in his pocket and pretends it's a gun, right? Well, apparently one robber thought that was a good idea and tried it out in an attempt to rob the Bank of America in Merced. But he forgot one thing—to hide his finger in his pocket. The index-indicating idiot aimed his uncovered finger, with his thumb cocked, of course, at the teller demanding money. The teller asked the robber to wait, then walked away. After some time the robber got tired of waiting. He unloaded his finger and walked out of the bank and crossed the street to another bank. This time he tried a different approach. He leaped over the counter and tried to wrestle the cash drawer key from a teller. An employee grabbed the key and told the thwarted thief to get out of there, according to Sgt. Gary Austin. The two-time loser was arrested shortly thereafter when he was discovered sitting in a clump of nearby shrubs. I guess now every time he sticks his finger up his nose it can be considered a suicide attempt.

Art for Art's Sake

Artist Trevor Corneliusen told sheriff's deputies that while camping in the Mojave Desert he had shackled his ankles together to draw a picture of his legs. According to a January 5, 2006, article in the *Los Angeles Times,* after Corneliusen had finished his sketch he realized he didn't have the key to the lock and had to hop around the desert for nearly twelve hours before finding his way to a gas station.

Stop Calling Me Names

Most people know that California's nickname is the Golden State but it has nothing to do with the gold rush of the mid-nineteenth century. The moniker was made official in 1968 and refers to the color of the California hillsides that, during the summer months, typically turn a golden brown.

What Goes Up . . .

The *Merced Sun-Star* reported on December 10, 2002, that police were called to investigate an incident involving a man who was taken to a Modesto hospital after his head was split open by a brick. Eyewitnesses quickly made it clear to investigators that the victim himself was actually as thick as a brick. Apparently the man tossed the brick into the air at 2:30 a.m. to see how high he could throw it and, as it was dark, lost sight of it until it clomped down on his head. Obviously the guy was a real blockhead.

Falling For Each Other

Television station KERO-TV in Bakersfield reported on September 27, 2007, that police were called to attend to a man and a woman who had fallen to the bottom of the Panorama Bluffs. The police ascertained from the couple that the man had attempted to toss his girlfriend over the 300-foot cliff but that she held on to him and they both fell. Police reported that it was the man who sustained the most injuries from the fall.

The city of Fallbrook, known as the Avocado Capital of the World, hosts an annual Avocado Festival. More avocados are grown in the region than in any other county in the nation.

If This Trailer's Rockin' . . .

A forty-three-year-old woman pulled out a .44-caliber Magnum revolver from a holster under her left arm and aimed it at a mouse scurrying across the floor of a small trailer that was traveling on Highway 20 in Potter Valley. According to a July 8, 2008, article in the *Santa Rosa Press Democrat,* the woman dropped the gun and it discharged. The bullet went through her kneecap, ricocheted off a set of keys dangling from the belt loop of a forty-two-year-old man who was in the moving trailer with her, tore a hole in his pants, grazed his groin, and finally came to rest in his coin pocket. The Mendocino County Sheriff's Office reported that the bullet had been admitted into evidence, and there was no word on the condition of the mouse.

The Missing Link

"I tell you, this was one weird case," said Lt. Ian Burrimond of the Fresno County Sheriff's Department. According to a September 6, 2008, article in the *Fresno Bee,* two men were awakened by an intruder who was rubbing spice mix on one of the men. When the second man jumped up, the intruder hit him in the head with an eight-inch sausage and then "the [intruder] ran out of the house wearing only a T-shirt, boxer shorts and socks, leaving behind his wallet with his I.D.," Burrimond said. Police quickly apprehended the suspect, twenty-two-year-old Antonio Vasquez, who was charged with robbery but then soon released citing insufficient evidence—you see, a dog had eaten the sausage used in the attack. "That's right," Burrimond said, "the dog ate the weapon."

Charity Begins at Home

An investigation conducted by the *Los Angeles Times* and reported in a July 6, 2008, article revealed that every single penny in donations made to 430 California charities was kept by the professional fund-raisers who solicited them. In fact, in 337 cases, the fund-raisers charged an additional fee on top of retaining 100 percent of the contributions (the charities did, however, receive each donor's name and address for future solicitations).

During a picnic of county probation officers in Yuba City, two thieves failed in their attempt to steal a barbecue grill— which was still hot.

You Can't Get There from Here

Ed Barney didn't like the cold weather at his new home in Santa Rosa, and after a fight with his wife, Arloween, he decided to set out on foot for the warmer climate of Arizona. He left behind his money and his cell phone, and apparently his sense of direction, too. According to a February 7, 2009, article in the *Santa Rosa Press,* Barney found his way onto a freight train he thought was headed south—but it was headed north. "He thought he was going to Arizona and he ended up in Oregon," Arloween said. Police traced Barney to Eugene, Oregon, by following his trail of ATM withdrawals. He was detained but no charges were filed, as he had committed no crime. But instead of heading back home, Barney purchased a bus ticket to Utah after he decided to visit his children.

Pumping Irony

During the state's budget crisis in July 2008, and as a way
to buy time for the legislature to pass a workable budget,
Governor Arnold Schwarzenegger fired approximately
10,000 temporary and part-time workers and ordered that
the salaries of 200,000 permanent employees be reduced
to the minimum wage of $6.55 an hour. A week later,
according to an August 8, 2008, article in the *Sacramento Bee,*
State Controller John Chiang said that the payrolls of the
permanent employees could not be altered because they
were written in the outdated COBOL computer language.
He went on to explain that the only state employees still
familiar with the antiquated code were the part-timers
whose position Schwarzenegger had just eliminated.

Cruise Control

An August 7, 2008, article from the Associated Press reported that a caravan of cars holding sixteen adults and ten children, all from California, was lost in the wilderness near the Grand Canyon. The drivers had been misguided by their GPS systems and now couldn't find their way back out. Fortunately, rescuers were able to talk them back to safety the next day by calling them on their cell phones.

Leaning to the Right and the Left

San Francisco Assemblyman Leland Yee discovered a foolproof way to be on both sides of an issue at the same time. Yee cosponsored a state bill requiring all semiautomatic handguns to leave a unique marking on every bullet fired, making it easier to trace the bullet back to the weapon. But in October 2006, when his bill came to the floor—Yee voted against it. That's right, he voted against his own bill and it failed by three votes. According to the law, since Yee was not the deciding vote, he was allowed to go back and officially change his vote to a yes. So technically Yee can say he cosponsored the bill and voted for it—when the reality is he cosponsored the bill and voted against it. Oh, Yee of little faith.

Well, I'll Be Horse-Whipped

Charley Darkey Parkhurst was just like any other stagecoach driver in the 1850s. Parkhurst was a "whip" on a six-horse coach and drove the treacherous San Jose–Santa Cruz route for the California Stage Lines until 1855. With one eye missing from a horse kick, a wad of tobacco in one cheek, and a trusted shotgun nearby, Parkhurst was the stereotype of the rugged stagecoach driver—except that Charley was really Charlotte. Few if any knew of Charlotte "Charley" Parkhurst's true identity until her death in 1879, when doctors discovered that she not only was a woman but also had previously given birth (no one knows what happened to the baby, assumed to have died at birth).

Don't Bet On It

After a lengthy court battle, the Me-Wuk tribe of the Buena
Vista Rancheria has received permission to build a casino
on its sixty-seven-acre reservation in Amador County. The
Buena Vista casino is scheduled to open in the fall of 2010
with 24,000 square feet of gambling, 950 slot machines,
and 20 game tables. According to a January 17, 2009,
article in the *Sacramento Bee,* the Me-Wuk tribe consists of
Rhonda Morningstar Pope, her husband, Marty, and their
five children, none of whom lives on the tribal land.

A burglar in Union City was startled
when the homeowner returned, and
the thief dashed out of the house and
over a fence. The man, who for some
reason was completely naked, was
quickly captured after his leap over
the fence landed him in the neighbor's
cactus garden.

The Butt of a Good Joke

San Luis Obispo Fire Department investigator John Madden ruled that a fire that destroyed the mobile home occupied by Bill Lewis and his mother, Chessie, was "strictly accidental." Lewis claimed that the fire, which caused $200,000 in damage, was started when his mother accidentally left a burning cigarette on the porch. Fortunately, the pair was not in the mobile home when the fire broke out, according to a January 27, 2009, article in the *San Luis Obispo Tribune,* as Lewis was taking his mother to the County Public Health Department for a meeting to help her quit smoking.

A Shaggy Dog Story

According to an April 13, 2006, article in the *San Francisco Chronicle,* the former executive director of the Humane Society in Oceanside, Stacy Steel, was arrested and charged with fraud. Steel was accused of using the organization's authority to buy 3,600 tablets of the prescription painkiller Vicodin, which she claimed were for her dog.

Oxnard resident Benny Zavala was convicted of animal abuse on October 25, 2002, for killing and dissecting his daughter's pet guinea pig because he believed the rodent was a government spy robot.

This Is Only a Test #1

The following are real answers received on exams given by the California Department of Transportation's driving school:

Q: Do you yield when a blind pedestrian is crossing the road?

A: What for? He can't see my license plate.

Q: Who has the right of way when four cars approach a four-way stop at the same time?

A: The pickup truck with the gun rack and the bumper sticker saying, GUNS DON'T KILL PEOPLE. I DO.

Q: When driving through fog, what should you use?

A: Your car.

Underhanded Pitch

Michael Oddenino, a lawyer in Arcadia, filed a $3 million lawsuit on behalf of his daughter against Don Riggio, who coached his daughter's high school softball team, claiming emotional distress. Oddenino's lawsuit stated that Riggio routinely called his daughter and her teammates names including "idiot" and "two-year-old." However, Oddenino struck out, according to a March 30, 2006, article in the Associated Press, when Superior Court Judge Jan Pluim dismissed the case.

A Rose By Any Other Name

"Crash," a pelican, got her nickname when she smashed into a car in Laguna Beach after becoming drunk on toxic algae. After undergoing foot and pouch surgery and a month's rehabilitation, she was set free in the waters of Corona del Mar, according to a July 21, 2006, article in the *Los Angeles Times*. But the bird crashed beak-first into some rocks before successfully lifting off.

A House Divided

California is such a large state, there has been talk since its inception of dividing it into two separate states. One of the stranger appeals to sever the state occurred on November 27, 1941, when motorists stopped at highway blockades on Route 99 outside of Yreka were handed fliers proclaiming the separate state of Jefferson. The flyer read in part:

State of Jefferson Proclamation of Independence

You are now entering Jefferson, the 49th State of the Union.

Jefferson is now in patriotic rebellion against the States of California and Oregon.

This State has seceded from California and Oregon this Thursday, November 27, 1941.

Patriotic Jeffersonians intend to secede each Thursday until further notice.

Born to Be Wild

The California Highway Patrol reported that fifty-year-old Richard Brooks of Concord claimed he was offended by a group of bikers who had skeletons on their Harley-Davidson jackets and what he perceived as their attempts to act tough. So he got into his car and charged at them waving a pool cue. Brooks, who according to a September 21, 2006, article in the *San Francisco Chronicle,* was allegedly intoxicated, then got out of his car and walked around behind it but apparently forgot to put the car in park—and it knocked him into traffic. The bikers risked their lives to pull him back to safety. Brooks was arrested on suspicion of assault with a deadly weapon and driving under the influence.

But How Do You Really Feel?

In February 2003, South Gate Mayor Xochitl Ruvalcaba stood in front of an estimated crowd of two hundred yelling and screaming people after she had been voted out of office by a special election on claims of corruption. To show her true feelings about being ousted, in part by her nemesis, Councilman Henry Gonzalez, the then thirty-year-old Ruvalcaba sucker-punched the councilman in the face. Gonzalez, it should be noted, was sixty-seven years old at the time and walked with the assistance of a cane.

Toad of Toad Hall

In 1995, after an overpass was built from North Davis to
South Davis, some citizens were concerned about the safety
of toads crossing that stretch of Interstate 80. The City of
Davis decided to build a toad tunnel (at a cost of $14,000)
to give the road-hopping amphibians safe passage. The
tunnel is twenty-one inches wide and eighteen inches tall
but the toads refused to use it until the city installed lights
inside the tunnel (originally the heat of the lights killed
many toads but that problem was rectified). The toads
weren't the only ones happy with their new tunnel—local
toad-eating birds were, too. A local postmaster constructed
a miniature village at the mouth of the tunnel (complete
with post office) to help the toads escape attack.

Smoke Gets In Your Eyes

On November 14, 2006, the San Francisco Board of Supervisors voted to instruct law officials to downgrade the smoking of marijuana to the city's lowest enforcement priority, according to the *San Francisco Chronicle*. The next day, Belmont became the first city in America to ban cigarette, cigar, and pipe smoking everywhere in the city limits, according to a November 15, 2006, article in the *San Mateo Daily Journal*. The ban includes all property, publicly or privately owned, including condominiums and even cars, but not detached, single-family homes.

From the
Mouths of Babes

Dominic Scott Kay, a Southern California filmmaker, filed a creative-control lawsuit, according to a January 26, 2007, article in the *Los Angeles Times,* against the producer of his short film, *Saving Angelo.* Kay alleged that Conroy Kanter "unfairly demanded creative control and distribution rights for" the film, which starred family friend Kevin Bacon. The suit was settled out of court with Kay receiving "full ownership and control" of the film, along with a $20,000 donation to Crusades for Animals. This seems like a normal day in LA—except that the filmmaker, Dominic Scott Kay, was ten years old.

Skating on Thin Ice

According to police, and reported in a January 31, 2007, article in the *Reno Gazette-Journal,* a fifty-year-old man who was ice-skating fell through the ice at Donner Lake near Truckee and drowned. The man was approximately one hundred yards off shore and was wearing skates on the bottom of two-foot-tall stilts when he crashed through the ice.

In the fall of 1992, Compton Mayor Walter R. Tucker III suggested that a local apartment building, where George and Barbara Bush lived for six months in 1949, qualified for national landmark status. Unfortunately, at the time of the proposal, authorities knew the apartment building as a local crack house.

What a Scream

The Scandia Family Fun Center in Sacramento has a thrill ride called the Screamer, which drops riders from 168 feet high, while spinning at 60 miles an hour, causing a pull of 3.5 Gs. But according to a March 31, 2007, report by KOVR-TV, since neighborhood residents complained about the noise, riders of the Screamer aren't allowed to scream. If someone is caught screaming, the ride is stopped and the rider is ejected (if they want to try again they have to go to the end of the line).

The Best Outsource of News

The Web site PasadenaNow.com, whose mission statement is to "serve the Pasadena, California-area community as a reliable online source of news, information, and entertainment," has announced it will go outside the community to fill the position of local government reporter. Not only out of the community but also out of the country. PasadenaNow.com announced in a May 10, 2007, Associated Press article that it would outsource its local government reporter position to India. According to the Web site's publisher, covering city hall politicians could be handled through telephone interviews and by watching live city council telecasts on the Internet.

Back to the Future

"If I would do another *Terminator* movie I would have Terminator travel back in time and tell Arnold not to have a special election."

Governor Arnold Schwarzenegger, on November 10, 2005,
concerning the special election he called in which all four of his
ballot initiatives were soundly defeated

Let Them Brows Cake

Miss King's Kitchens of Sherman, the maker of YA-HOO! cakes, sued Yahoo! Inc. of Sunnyvale, an Internet search engine service. The bakery claimed that the similarities in the companies' names and logos could confuse consumers into believing that Miss King's products are really the products of the software company. To ensure that no one mistakes pastries and other delicacies for a Web browser, there is a disclaimer at the bottom of Miss King's Kitchens' Web site: "Not affiliated with Yahoo! Inc., the search engine company."

A Real Blast

The *Los Angeles Times* reported on February 24, 2003, that thirty-three-year-old Luis Chavez was arrested at his condominium in Cypress after he, for reasons unknown, deliberately set off aerial fireworks in his bedroom—resulting in $135,000 in damage.

Don't Look, Ethel!

A brief cold snap in San Jose in January 2007 put a halt to a lot of outdoor activities. Especially noteworthy was the absence of a middle-aged man who liked to jog naked at the Fremont Older Open Space Preserve. The man was reported several times before Jack Frost bit at probably more than his nose. He was occasionally sighted wearing only glasses, shoes, and, if it was a cool day, a black tam hat. According to a January 26, 2007, Associated Press article, Sue Bowdoin, who encountered the nude jogger twice while riding her horse, said, "I think he has a screw loose."

Update:

In February 2007 the nude jogger was identified as Silicon Valley engineer Darryl Delacruz, who paid a $95 fine and apologized for his actions. The president of the Midpeninsula Rangers Peace Officers Association, Kerry Carlson, was reported as saying, "We don't see it as appropriate behavior. A significant number of people feel uncomfortable with a nude person running around."

Up in Smoke

Long Beach police spokeswoman Nancy Pratt said, "It will then be up to the DA to determine what, if any, charges to file. But we believe that what he did was serious." She was talking about fifty-year-old Haouy Nguyen, who went inside Long Beach City Hall, doused himself with gasoline, and set himself on fire. Nguyen was quickly extinguished by a security guard and suffered burns over 20 percent of his body. Although the true reasons for his actions were unclear, said Pratt, "We think the motive was probably suicide." According to an April 20, 2007, article in the *Los Angeles Times,* prosecutors had to decide whether to charge Nguyen with arson.

The More the Merrier

Wanda Langstom, an eighty-one-year-old resident of
Wilmington, was taken to a local hospital for treatment
of multiple animal bites. The Los Angeles Department of
Animal Services searched Langstom's home and found
about 120 rats and 35 other animals, mostly in cages, that
Langstom claimed were all her pets. "Langstom basically
became overwhelmed at how quickly the rats reproduced,"
said an animal control officer. "She said it just started with
two but it got out of hand." According to a June 6, 2007,
article in the *Los Angeles Times,* the animals were removed
from Langstom's home, taken to a shelter, and put up for
adoption.

A Real Cliff-Hanger

An eighteen-year-old woman, Kimberly Kiesz, was walking on top of the cliffs in Palos Verdes Estates when one of her flip-flops flipped off her foot and flopped over the cliff. "She went to retrieve it and lost her footing and ended up grabbing hold onto the base of some shrubbery with her feet dangling over the edge," said Police Chief Dan Dreiling. Five police officers arrived at the scene, according to an August 10, 2007, article in the *Santa Monica Daily Breeze,* and owing to the precarious nature of the situation (a two hundred–foot drop) formed a human chain and saved Kiesz. "We didn't rescue the flip-flop," Dreiling said. "It remains on the scene."

Out of the Rough

According to an April 3, 2007, article in the *San Diego Union-Tribune,* Bishop Michael Babin, a leader of Genesis Ministries International in Oceanside for twenty-five years, was nominated for a Martin Luther King Jr. Civic Award in 2005. The article wasn't about his award, however. It concerned his arrest (along with his son) on the charge of beating a golfer unconscious after they accused the man of stealing the bishop's golf ball at the Oceanside Municipal Golf Course.

"THIS IS THE WORST DISASTER IN CALIFORNIA SINCE I WAS ELECTED."

Governor Pat Brown, referring to a local flood

Smile!

Pacifica police ruled out homicide in the case of a forty-three-year-old man who died while having sex with an exotic dancer. It was discovered that the man had set up a video camera to record his tryst and the tape showed that he suffered a heart attack, according to a May 9, 2007, article in the *San Francisco Chronicle*. However, the video also showed the woman using drugs before the couple got down to business and she was arrested and sentenced to a year in jail.

Life Imitating Art

A seventeen-year-old boy was seriously injured when he plummeted about seventy-five feet onto some rocks at Mount Diablo State Park in the San Francisco Bay Area. According to a June 12, 2007, article in the *San Jose Mercury News,* the boy had asked his friends to videotape him jumping over the rail (thus giving the illusion that he had jumped) in order to post the video on his MySpace Web page.

The Wrong Side of the Tracks

The *Oakland Tribune* reported on November 16, 2007, about a thirty-one-year-old man who usually crossed two train tracks to get to a hole in a fence as his shortcut to work. Unfortunately, the report was about the last time he took his shortcut—this time talking on his cell phone. Scott Slaughter waited for one train to pass but apparently was so distracted by his conversation that he didn't see the second Amtrak train traveling at 70 mph.

About a week later, sixteen-year-old Daniel Segundo ducked under a crossing gate in San Leandro while chatting on his cell phone and was also struck by an Amtrak train.

(San Francisco Chronicle, December 7, 2007)

Unfit Counterfeiter

In Los Angeles, Tekle Zigetta was arrested and pled guilty to charges of attempting to smuggle $250 billion into the country. According to a March 15, 2006, article in Reuters, customs agents discovered 250 bills each with a denomination of $1 billion bearing the likeness of Grover Cleveland. (The highest denomination of U.S. paper currency is $100.)

What's Eating You?

The Donner party, led by George Donner, comprised a group of eighty-seven people who were caught up in California's gold rush. In the winter of 1846, after several setbacks in their journey, they found themselves caught in the heaviest snowfall in the Sierra Nevada in thirty years, with more than twenty feet of snow. Only forty of the original travelers survived—and it was eventually reported that a number of them survived only by eating other members of the party. Donner Lake and Donner Pass are both named after their ill-fated journey.

What's the Buzz All About?

Since 2002 Marin County has been certifying and awarding businesses that excel in environmental awareness with its Green Business Program. According to an August 15, 2007, article in the *Marin Independent Journal,* one of the most recent recipients was Pleasures of the Heart. The San Rafael sex-toy and lingerie store qualified in part because it sells erotic underwear made of organic bamboo fabric and good-for-the-environment rechargeable vibrators.

There's a Roach in My Chicken

A man placed his order at a Kentucky Fried Chicken drive-through in Mill Valley and proceeded to the window. He then requested extra biscuits and was shocked when he got two bags of marijuana instead. The stunned customer gave the bags back to the employee, drove off, and called police. The police arrested the twenty-six-year-old worker at the restaurant. I guess the guy's brain was already extra-crispy.

"All of a sudden, we see riots, we see protests, we see people clashing. The next thing we know, there is injured or there is dead people. We don't want to get to that extent."

Governor Arnold Schwarzenegger, on the dangers posed if the courts continued to perform gay marriages, which are against existing state laws, on NBC's *Meet the Press*, February 22, 2004

Just a Lucky Coincidence

In 2005, Rep. Ken Calvert (R-CA) and his real estate
partner, Woodrow Harpole Jr., paid $550,000 for four acres
of land a few miles south of the March Air Force Reserve
Base. Less than a year after their purchase, and without
making any improvements to the land, they sold the
property for $985,000. Why the sudden increase in value?
Because Congress had earmarked $8 million to expand
a freeway interchange sixteen miles from the property
and secured an additional $1.5 million for commercial
development in the area adjacent to the airfield. Who
pushed for the earmarks? You guessed it, Rep. Ken Calvert.
I'm not connecting any dots here—I'm just telling you
where the dots are.

A Display of Passion

A burglar alarm summoned police to a western boot store in Bakersfield. When police passed in front of the large display window they noticed there was more in there than just hand-tooled leather boots: A naked couple had gone from hand-tooled to knocking boots. An officer tapped on the window to alert the two booty-bouncing burglars they were getting the boot. The couple took to their heels but were quickly apprehended and charged with burglary, resisting an officer, assault on an officer, and indecent exposure. The two bootlicks admitted they had broken into the store to get out of the rain and then ducked into a "hidden" place to have sex. If the shoe fits, wear it—but if the boot fits, wear it out.

Getting Shortchanged

Police in Burlingame were called out to investigate a
burglary at the Towles Coffee Shop. The store's owners
kept any valuables locked up after closing and the burglar
had a hard time finding anything worth stealing. Police
surmised that he made several attempts at breaking into a
locked metal cabinet but was ultimately unsuccessful (the
cabinet contained toilet paper anyway). Finally, not wanting
to leave empty-handed and be the laughingstock of the
burglar community, he stole the money from the "penny
cup," which was located next to the cash register. The thief
got away with about thirty cents. I hope he didn't spend it
all in one place.

1995 FEDERAL BUDGET:
$384,948 FOR THE DEPARTMENT OF LABOR
TO COUNT HOW MANY DOGS AND CATS
LIVE IN VENTURA COUNTY.

The Check's in the Jail

A man in Auburn was arrested and charged with burglary, forgery, and passing bad checks after purchasing $267 worth of supplies from an office store. The man had painstakingly printed bogus checks, complete with false bank account numbers that could be successfully scanned through any store's check identification system. So where did our crafty counterfeiter go wrong? For some unknown reason the man had printed his full and proper name and address on every check. Pay to the Order Of: Idiot.

RIGHT OUTSIDE THE CAPITOL BUILDING, IN 2001, REP. TOM LANTOS (D-CA) DROVE OVER A THIRTEEN-YEAR-OLD BOY'S FOOT AND THEN LEFT THE SCENE.

It Doesn't Always Pay to Advertise

An inmate at the San Mateo County minimum-security jail decided he'd had enough of prison life and simply walked away during work release. He got a little tired of walking and stopped at a pay phone to call a friend to come pick him up. Try as he might, the convict couldn't remember his friend's phone number, so he called directory assistance, 411, to get it. Unfortunately, he accidentally dialed 911 instead and quickly hung up the phone. The police sent out a cruiser to check on the 911 hang-up anyway and found the man still in the phone booth and still wearing his prison shirt with the words "Property of San Mateo County Honor Camp" written on it. "They could see it through the top of his jacket," said Sheriff's Lt. Larry Boss. At least when they took the inmate back to celebrate his reunion with his fellow prisoners he was already dressed for the occasion.

What's in a Name?

The Associated Press reported on March 29, 1998, about
a study conducted by the University of California at San
Diego that gave a lot of people an initial concern. The
research disclosed that people whose initials spell out
positive words live longer than those whose names spell
out negative words. "It's a little tiny depressant to be called
PIG, or a little tiny boost to your esteem to be called ACE
or WOW," said psychologist Nicholas Christenfeld, who
along with two others coined their hypothesis the "Theory
of Deadly Initials." People whose initials spelled out words
like VIP or GOD lived an average of 4.48 years longer
than the control group, whose initials had no distinctive
qualities, while the people with initials such as DIE or
BUM died 2.8 years sooner than the control group.

Better Living Through Chemicals

When city officials in Aliso Viejo, in Orange County, heard that Styrofoam containers were produced using the dangerous chemical "dihydrogen monoxide" they jumped into action. The concerned and socially responsible councilors proposed going before the city legislature to outlaw the potentially deadly substance from within the city boundaries—when they discovered something. The embarrassed officials, the Associated Press reported in a March 15, 2004, article, soon learned that dihydrogen monoxide, or H_2O for short, is the chemical formula for water. "It's embarrassing," said City Manager David J. Norman. "We had a paralegal who did bad research."

Getting into a Real Jam

Researchers from Humboldt State University, as reported in the *Dallas Morning News* (August 7, 1995), announced that they had discovered chemical compounds that could kill several common types of bacteria, such as propionibacterium acnes (that causes acne), and certain fungi, including one that causes athlete's foot. The researchers discovered this naturally occurring chemical in the toe jam of black-tailed deer.

On March 18, 1848, the *California Star* reported that the non-native population of San Francisco was 812 (575 males, 177 females, and 60 children). By December 31, 1849, the population had skyrocketed and was estimated at 100,000, including 35,000 who came by sea, 3,000 sailors who deserted ships, and 42,000 who arrived overland.

Yellow Dog Democrat

The residents of one small California town didn't think it odd when they saw their mayor begging for beef jerky, sniffing trees, rolling in the dirt, running after sticks, or even standing around with his tongue hanging out and drooling. That's because their mayor was a Labrador retriever and, though this may or may not be unusual behavior for a politician, it is acceptable when the politician is a dog.

Bosco was elected mayor of Sunol in 1983 and served his community faithfully for eleven years, until his death in 1994. The town—which had a population of about a thousand people at the time of his demise—is thirty miles southeast of San Francisco and fifteen miles north of San Jose.

The Original Big Macs

We've all heard the name Ray Kroc before, right? He's the guy who founded McDonald's. But if he was the founder, why didn't he call his franchise Kroc's—or even McKroc's? Well, obviously no one would eat at a restaurant named McKroc's, but the real reason is that he wasn't the restaurant's founder. Richard and Maurice McDonald, who opened their first drive-in restaurant near Pasadena, started McDonald's in 1940. In 1954, Kroc, who was a milkshake-machine salesman, bought the franchise rights from the brothers and eventually acquired the McDonald's name for $14 million, completing his buyout in 1961. So saying that Ray Kroc founded McDonald's is, well, a bunch of crock.

This Is a Great Place for a Stickup

Police pulled over sixty-four-year-old Arthur Cheney near Marysville after a report that his car had been spotted at the scene of a recent bank robbery. According to a December 12, 2007, article in the *Marin Independent Journal,* Cheney was arrested after police discovered a yellow "sticky" note stuck to the center console of his car with "Robbery 100s and 50s only." A spokesman for the police department exclaimed, "We call that a clue."

Don't Box Me In

Charles Loeb, an aspiring actor determined to become a movie star, mailed himself in 1929 from Chicago to a film studio in Culver City in a box labeled "Statue–handle with care." He arrived almost dead but told police he was happy because he had finally made it through the gates of a major studio.

A forty-seven-year-old man in Aptos died after he lost his balance while removing his pants, hopped over to a window on the second story of his home, and accidentally fell out.

Sacramento Bee, August 2, 2002

The Fat of the Land

The getaway is one of the most important parts of any successful bank robbery. One needs to have the proper vehicle ready and running, make sure there's gas in the tank, have a fairly well-planned escape route, etc. But one robber thought he would just wing his escape or, actually, foot it. A man in Fremont had accomplished the first part of a bank robbery—the initial "Give me all the money" bit. He took the money and headed out the door intending to run "wee, wee, wee" all the way home. Passersby, however, had a different idea when they saw the man exit the bank with the money and gave chase. After less than a block the robber gave up his sprint to freedom and slowed down to a leisurely walk. Was he confident he had gotten away? Nope. You see, the suspect was only five feet six inches tall and weighed well over three hundred pounds. Our rotund robber needed a rest and the sentencing judge was more than glad to give him several years to catch his breath.

A Real Dick

"Wanted: Congressional candidate with no previous political experience to defeat a man who has represented the district in the House for 10 years," read an ad that appeared in several Southern California newspapers in 1946. "Any young man, resident of district, preferably a veteran, fair education, may apply for the job." The ad wasn't a joke. The Republican Party, hoping to find a maverick politician to defeat incumbent Congressman Jerry Voorhis, had placed it. To everyone's surprise a maverick politician did answer the ad—and did go on to defeat Voorhis for California's 12th congressional district. The want-ad answering politician's name: Richard M. Nixon.

Go West, Young Man

It's assumed that sunny California became the home to early filmmakers because it's, well, sunny. Motion picture cameras of the day required a lot of light and it's a lot less expensive to shoot outdoors than in a studio. But these pioneers of the picture show weren't just looking for a place in the sun—they were also looking for a place to hide. You see, Thomas Edison owned the patent on the film camera and these fringe filmmakers were infringing on Edison's patent. Southern California became the perfect location because it was as far away from Edison's lawyers as one could get and still stay in the United States, and if the lawyers "went west," it was a simple matter to pack up those cameras and escape to Mexico.

Bush League Company

The Pacific Gas & Electric Company was on trial in
Nevada City in 2000, charged with "failing to trim
vegetation around power lines." The trial was delayed
for more than thirty minutes when the town's power was
accidentally cut off—a tree branch had fallen and knocked
down a power line. It's events like these that strengthen my
belief in God—and show that he's got a sense of humor.

"Look at this!"

The classic final words from a thirty-two-year-old man from
Santa Cruz who wanted his friends to see him dangling precariously
from a hotel balcony—moments before he fell to his death
(*Santa Cruz Sentinel*, October 5, 2002)

Too Much Information

"It's the most difficult [decision] I've made in my entire life, except the one I made in 1978 when I decided to get a bikini wax."

—Arnold Schwarzenegger announcing his candidacy for California governor on the *Tonight Show with Jay Leno*, August 6, 2003

"WOMEN PREFER DEMOCRATS TO MEN."

Representative Tony Coelho, Democrat

Look, Up in the Sky, It's a Bird . . .

In November 1977 it wasn't raining cats and dogs; it was actually raining birds. According to accounts, approximately five hundred dead and dying blackbirds and pigeons dropped on the streets and sidewalks of San Luis Obispo over a period of several hours. As no local spraying had occurred, authorities had no explanation for why the birds had died en masse over their town—giving rise to a different meaning for the phrase "bird droppings."

Color-Coded Cops

Traffic Commissioner Matt Flynn of Laguna Beach decided to dismiss a man's speeding ticket in October 1993 because the cop's motorcycle was the wrong color. According to state law, all police vehicles must be painted either black and white or just white—but this officer's motorcycle was painted blue and white.

Dream a Little Dream

Thirty-one-year-old Sari Zayed sued city hall in Davis after she was hauled into court for snoring too loudly. Zayed shares a common wall with a neighbor, Chris Doherty, and when her snoring kept him awake, Doherty called police. A California noise enforcement officer issued Zayed a $50 citation in 1994 at 1:30 a.m. The citation was eventually dismissed but then Zayed filed a lawsuit seeking damages of $24,000 for stress, lost wages, and other losses (loss of sleep wasn't mentioned). The lawsuit was finally settled for $13,500 in March 1995. "I'm happy that we settled out of court," Zayed said. "But as far as this being truly over, it will never be truly over until the city stops doing stupid things." I wouldn't lose any sleep over it, Ms. Zayed.

Frozen in History

On an unseasonably cold San Francisco night in 1905, as the story goes, eleven-year-old Frank Epperson left a glass filled with powdered soda, water, and a stirring stick on his back porch. The next morning Epperson found the frozen treat on a stick and it gave him an idea. In 1924 he finally got around to patenting "a handled, frozen confection or ice lollipop," which he called the "Epsicle." At the insistence of his children, he later changed the name of the flavored treat to "Popsicle" (a combination of the word "pop," after their dad, and "icicle," after the frozen confection).

Boxer Shorts

"Greg's naked body was long and elegant, his embrace enveloped her utterly, and they meshed with ease and grace. He smelled good too, faintly and astringently of aftershave. He was clinging to her as if he'd never let her go, it was all so easy and right."

Excerpt from the novel *A Time to Run* by Sen. Barbara Boxer (D-CA)

Justice Is Served

In March 1995, Jerry Williams, considered a habitual criminal under California's "three strikes" law, was sentenced to twenty-five years to life in prison. What was the crime that put Williams away for good? He stole a slice of pizza from a group of children on a Redondo Beach pier.

A sixty-six-year-old woman from Menlo Park, Mrs. Jessie Brockman, was thwarted in her attempt to commit suicide, according to a September 27, 2003, article from the Associated Press. Brockman had a heart attack and died of natural causes before she could pull the trigger.

To Thine Own Self Be Sued

Curtis Gokey of Lodi City was surprised to find out that a city dump truck had smashed his car, so he sued city hall for $3,600. It's not surprising that someone would sue the city in a case like this—except that the driver of the dump truck was Gokey himself. Gokey admitted that he was the one driving the truck but still felt that he was entitled to be compensated for the damage to his own car. After the city refused his claim, Gokey's wife, Rhonda, tried to sue the city and even upped the damages to $4,800—but was told that one spouse can't sue the other "for damage to community property." According to an Associated Press article from March 16, 2006, the city council denied her claim, too.

Hit or Stay?

Toshi Van Blitter decided to take the biggest gamble of her life and sued Harrah's casinos in Las Vegas, Nevada. Blitter, of El Macero, played blackjack at two of the casinos and racked up $350,000 in debt. Since she hadn't done well at cards, she tried her hand at another suit—a lawsuit. In 1985, Blitter filed to have her debts canceled, claiming that Harrah's was negligent. For what? Blitter claimed Harrah's should have told her that she was an incompetent blackjack player or suggested that she take classes on playing the game. Her case went bust, however, when two federal judges dismissed her claim.

This Is Only a Test #2

The following are more real answers received on exams given by the California Department of Transportation's driving school:

Q: **What are some points to remember when passing or being passed?**

A: Make eye contact and wave "hello" if he/she is cute.

Q: **What is the difference between a flashing red traffic light and a flashing yellow traffic light?**

A: The color.

Q: **How do you deal with heavy traffic?**

A: Heavy psychedelics.

Foot Patrol

Some idiots steal for fun and the thrill, some because they can't help themselves, some for no reason at all, and some out of necessity. At a Wal-Mart store in San Diego, a man was confronted by a security guard for allegedly stealing six packages of Dr. Scholl's corn remover. The two got into a short scuffle and the man got away—but not very far. According to a police spokesman, "The suspect was unable to run away because of the corns on his feet." The police never made fun of the man's corns because that would be too callous.

"THE PUBLIC DOESN'T CARE ABOUT FACTS AND FIGURES."

• • • •

California gubernatorial candidate Arnold Schwarzenegger,
to a gathering of several hundred reporters after the inaugural meeting
of his "Economic Recovery Council," August 20, 2003

What's Got Your Goat?

The *Taylor Crop Newsletter* reported that a grievance had been filed against Mills College, an eight hundred–student women's institution, by the Teamsters Local 70 in Oakland citing a violation of an agreement with the union. The Teamsters claimed the school contracted non-union workers to clear about forty acres of poison ivy–infested land and they demanded restitution. The union stipulated that the school be forced to award back pay for the members who lost out on the work or, as an alternative, that the five hundred non-union workers who cleared the field be forced to join Local 70. The five hundred non-union individuals in question were unable to answer these charges, as they were–goats. Seriously, the five hundred goats that cleared the land were hired from a company called "Goats R Us."

Betting on a Long Shot

A Marin County woman is fighting her credit card companies in their attempt to recover more than $70,000 in charges. The woman became addicted to gambling over the Internet and ran up credit card charges on both her Visa and MasterCard but won't even pay the minimum due. Not only has she refused to pay the credit card companies, but she has also filed a countersuit against them claiming that because gambling is illegal in California, the credit card companies shouldn't have allowed the charges to go through in the first place. Think she'll be successful? Don't bet on it.

Quick-Change Artist

A man in Eureka was caught on surveillance cameras stealing coins from a soda vending machine. Apparently thirsty after stealing all the cold, hard cash, the man put some of the change back into the machine to get a drink. The soda machine malfunctioned and didn't dispense his drink. Outraged at the machine and how it had "eaten his money," the thief—still caught on tape, mind you—wrote a note on the machine with his name and phone number and the amount of money the machine owed him. I wonder if during his arraignment he paid his bond entirely in quarters.

While golfing, Tom Stafford of Mission Viejo sliced the ball too hard to the left, causing it to ricochet off a steel pole and crack him in the forehead. He sued the golf course for damages and in November 1993 won an $8,500 settlement.

Taking a Powder

California, 1994. It was a daring plan. It required catlike grace, the cunning of a mastermind, split-second timing, and flawless execution—unfortunately, it was organized by a partnership between federal and state governments. The plan was to tempt alleged big-time drug traffickers with two hundred pounds of cocaine, courtesy of Uncle Sam. Once they took the bait, state and federal authorities would swoop down on the bad guys, make the news, and make the streets safe. The plan didn't include the bad guys getting away with the cocaine—but that's what happened, putting $4 million in premium-grade cocaine out on the street. And they say it's the thought that counts.

Driver, Move That Bus!

In the show *Extreme Makeover: Home Edition,* a group of designers descend on a house and transform it while the owners are away—and that's sort of what happened to one residence in Cool. Terence Michael Dean was arrested for breaking and entering and making some bold design choices. He had left all the faucets running, arranged packages of meat in the bathtub and sink, crafted a shrine of Buddha on a bongo drum, scattered a trail of potting soil from a walkway to the shrine, put teddy bears in three plant stands, dug up nearly one hundred plants in the yard, and left a piece of paper floating in a cup of water with "I love cherry" written on it. In the September 24, 2006, edition of the *Mountain Democrat* newspaper, the homeowner said that when he arrived home he saw Dean escape clothed only in a sheet.

Up in Smoke

An eighty-year-old man, whose name was not released by the press, was accidentally killed in Downey while seeking revenge on his neighbors. The man, who neighbors said "hated everybody," was attempting to put an explosive device in a neighbor's home but carelessly set his arm on fire while trying to light it. According to the January 9, 2006, Associated Press article about the incident, the fire on his arm ignited the fuse and the bomb exploded, killing him instantly.

A taste test turned violent in Pomona when James Howle and Kevin Williams stabbed each other in a disagreement over which of their two alcoholic drinks tasted better.

KNBC-TV, Los Angeles, October 21, 2003

Now It Makes Sense

Tenses, Gender, and Number: For the purpose of the rules and regulations contained in this chapter, the present tense includes the past and future tenses, and the future, the present; the masculine gender includes the feminine, and the feminine, the masculine, and the singular includes the plural, and the plural the singular.

Excerpt from the revised (1973) state code for the California Department of Consumer Affairs

Two Dumb Bells

The alarm sounded at the Buffum-Downtown YMCA in Long Beach and the police arrived within five minutes. They soon discovered two men trying to steal six forty-five-pound barbells that were loaded in a rickety shopping cart. Too bad the two thieves were two ninety-five-pound weaklings, because the shopping cart kept tipping over on them as they tried to escape. "They weren't even very big guys," said Tim Hardy, physical education director at the gym. When the police cornered them, the two thieves struggled to lift the barbells into a trash bin. They were quickly arrested and placed on $5,000 bond each. There was no explanation why the two dumbbells wanted the six barbells—they were only worth about sixty cents a pound. Maybe they knew they would eventually be arrested and wanted to tone up before going to prison.

Behind Closed Doors

The California Board of Education decided to meet in secret to decide whether it should meet in secret. That's right. No one was told what the second meeting would be about—it was secret. But according to law they have to announce if they are going to meet in secret—even if it's a secret. The law goes like this: Government Code Section 11126(q)2(a) . . . "The California State Board of Education reserves the right to meet in closed session pursuant to Government Code Section 11126(q)2(a) to determine whether the facts or circumstances authorize it to meet in closed session pursuant to Government Code Section 11126(q)2(a)." I think if the Board of Education has something to say, it should share it with the whole class.

Jeffrey Lee Daniels of Barstow admitted to accepting $10 from a fifty-eight-year-old male acquaintance for the opportunity to sleep in the same bed with him. But Daniels said he was shocked and incensed when the man touched him "in the area of his butt" and he wound up killing the man.

Victorville *Daily Press*, December 5, 2002

Legal Nutcases

The Association of Community Organizations for Reform Now (ACORN), an activist group that fought for legislation to increase the minimum hourly wage to $5.75, filed a lawsuit in California, pleading with the court to be exempt from paying its own employees the state's current minimum hourly wage of $4.24. In its legal brief, the group argued for exemption on the grounds that "the more that ACORN must pay each individual outreach worker . . . the fewer outreach workers it will be able to hire." Looks like the ACORN doesn't fall too far from the tree.

A Novel Name

The book *Las Sergas de Esplandián* ("The Adventures of Esplandián") is a romance novel written by Garci Rodríguez de Montalvo at the beginning of the 1500s. The story partly involves a fictional island named California, known by sailors not only for its abundance of pearls and gold but also because its inhabitants were a tribe of black Amazonian women. The women allowed men ashore only for the purpose of procreation and would kill any man who set foot on their island for any other reason. When early explorers discovered a peninsula off western Mexico teeming with pearls they named it California—and the name has stuck ever since.

Up a Tree

Julia "Butterfly" Hill made her place in history by making her home in a six hundred–year-old, 180-foot-tall redwood tree nicknamed "Luna." On December 10, 1997, the twenty-three-year-old woman scaled the tree in Humboldt County to protest the Pacific Lumber Company's logging of the last of the redwood forests. She stayed perched in the tree for 738 days before finally climbing down on December 18, 1999. She garnered a great deal of media attention and not only saved a number of redwood trees but also was awarded the Courage of Conscience award on October 31, 2002.

A Town Called Allensworth

When he retired from the U.S. Army in 1906, Lt. Col. Allen Allensworth was the highest-ranking African American commissioned officer in the U.S. military. Two years later, Allensworth wanted to establish a city where blacks could live the American dream and be free from racial discrimination, so he founded the town of Allensworth just north of Bakersfield, in Tulare County. Unfortunately, the dream of the city died when its founder died unexpectedly on September 14, 1914, and the town's inhabitants slowly drifted away. Today the Colonel Allensworth State Historic Park commemorates his city of hope.

Gray on the Concept

Governor Gray Davis insisted on March 14, 2000, that judges he's appointed to the bench should reflect Davis's views or resign. "I've let every judge know that, while they have to follow the law . . . they're there because I appointed them, and they need to keep faith with my electoral mandate," said Davis at the National Governors Association conference in Washington, D.C., according to an article in the *San Diego Union-Tribune*. "All my appointees," he continued, "including judges, have to, more or less, reflect the views I've expressed in my election," he said. "Otherwise, democracy doesn't work." Fortunately, the recall election in 2003 showed that democracy did work and voters told Gray "Hasta la vista, baby!"

AC/DC

Beckman Research Institute, a research facility affiliated with the City of Hope National Medical Center in Duarte, announced in a September 16, 2002, article in *New Scientist* that it had genetically engineered flies to change their sexual orientation. Scientists revealed they were able to temporarily change the flies from heterosexual to homosexual simply by increasing the external temperature to higher than 86 degrees.

Home Is Where the Pipe Is

Some two hundred people left homeless during the winter of 1932–1933 during the Great Depression found a home away from home in six-foot-long concrete sewer pipes. The small makeshift town that the pipe-dwellers called "Miseryville" and the newspapers, "Pipe City," was at the foot of Nineteenth Avenue in Oakland. The tenants used cardboard or burlap to cover the opening to the pipes and did the best they could to make themselves comfortable inside—they made communal mulligan stew from discarded produce from a nearby grocery wholesaler's garbage.

"POWER-MONGERING MEN WITH SHORT PENISES."

• • • •

California State Assembly Speaker Doris Allen's opinion,
shortly before her resignation, of her critics

Blue Jay Way

California is full of folklore, legend, and larger-than-life characters, including the Naked Guy. While attending the University of California at Berkeley in 1990, Luis Andrew Martinez (aka the Naked Guy) was an activist who fought the established norm of wearing clothes in public. He claimed he reached his naked nirvana by reading the works of philosopher Henry David Thoreau and actually went door to door asking neighbors if they minded his nudity. There was no ordinance at that time against public nudity and Martinez used his celebrity status to appear on TV talk shows and even posed in *Playgirl* magazine. His reign of baring it all ended in 1993 when the city finally adopted an antinudity ordinance.

Unfortunately, the Naked Guy didn't have a happy ending (sorry for the pun). After he was arrested for a fight in January 2006, thirty-three-year-old Martinez was found dead in his Santa Clara County Jail cell in San Jose with a plastic bag tied around his head.

Home Sweet Home

Most states have opulent executive mansions where the governor and his family reside during their tenure, and California is no different. Built in Sacramento in 1877, the mansion has thirty rooms with French mirrors and fireplaces made from Italian marble with chandeliers hanging from the fourteen-foot ceilings. But there's one thing different about California's executive mansion—the governor doesn't live there. In fact, the last governor to reside at the mansion was Ronald Reagan. That's because when Jerry Brown became governor he decided to sell the mansion and turned it into a state park.

"GAY MARRIAGE SHOULD BE BETWEEN A MAN AND A WOMAN."

· · · ·

Governor Arnold Schwarzenegger, in a radio interview with
Sean Hannity, *New York Daily News,* August 29, 2003

Knees Up, Mother Brown

"Her skirt was very short, and Josh found himself mesmerized by her perfectly shaped, silken legs with kneecaps that reminded him of golden apples—he couldn't remember having been captivated by kneecaps before—and her lustrous thighs. He tore his eyes away from Bianca's legs with the utmost difficulty."

Excerpt from the novel *A Time to Run* by Sen. Barbara Boxer (D-CA)

Standard Equipment

The driver of a white Mazda was arrested in Redondo Beach and charged with drunken driving. The police had noticed the car driving erratically down the Pacific Coast Highway, but what really caught their eye was the upper half of a traffic light pole lying across the car's hood. When pulled over by police, the man explained that the pole "came with the car when I bought it."

It's Hammer Time!

An October 16, 2007, article in the *San Francisco Chronicle* tells the strange story of Jayantibhai Patel, who was arrested in Foster City after he cracked his father in the head with a hammer. Patel admitted he had hit his father in the head with a hammer hard enough to require hospitalization but said that was exactly the point. The fifty-seven-year-old Patel told police he wanted to put his father in a nursing home and believed he could only be assigned one if his father was in the hospital—so he made sure his father was in a hospital.

Where's Mr. Noodle?

It's not unusual for politicians to ask celebrities to speak to Congress about topics on which they are knowledgeable or feel passionate. So when Rep. Duke Cunningham (R-CA) wanted to find an instantly recognizable superstar to speak on the importance of music education, he didn't go to Hollywood Boulevard or K Street—he went to Sesame Street. Cunningham asked the beloved furry red creature Elmo to testify at the Capitol, and Elmo said, "Elmo be happy to." One political analyst who witnessed the event said, "Elmo has higher poll ratings than most members of Congress. They like to be in his reflective glory"—though it's hard to take advice from a felt puppet that has someone's hand stuck up its butt.

Déjà Vu

Howard Shanholtzer allegedly stole security cameras and
made his getaway in his white Mitsubishi pickup. Fearing
that police would be on the lookout for his truck, he
ditched it and allegedly stole another vehicle. According
to a May 24, 2008, article in the *Orange County Register,*
Shanholtzer was arrested even though he had swapped
vehicles—but for reasons unknown, the vehicle that
Shanholtzer stole was another white Mitsubishi pickup
truck.

He's a Real Mother, All Right

According to a June 11, 2006, article in the *Los Angeles Times,* Michael Cohn, a Los Angeles psychologist, filed a lawsuit against the Los Angeles Angels baseball team. The lawsuit alleged discrimination because Cohn didn't receive one of the red nylon tote bags the team was giving away to women on "Family Sunday" to celebrate Mother's Day.

Michael Schoop tried to convince a judge in Oakland that the reason he had child pornography on his computer was that he had accidentally downloaded them while searching the Internet for asparagus recipes— the judge didn't buy it.

San Francisco Chronicle, October 28, 2003

Say "Cheese!"

A series of photographs by Jill Greenberg caused controversy during its Los Angeles exhibit. Greenberg's "End Time" showed twenty-seven portraits of children between the ages of two and three with their faces contorted in emotional distress. Greenberg said she evoked the sad reactions from some of the subjects by offering them candy and then taking it away. The *Guardian* reported on July 26, 2006, that the artist admitted the photos were "upsetting" but denied accusations that they were child abuse. Greenberg said her photographs were created to express her frustration with both the Bush administration and Christian fundamentalism in America.

Limp Blimp

It certainly wasn't a good year for a cameraman aboard the 192-foot-long Goodyear blimp after it got away from the ground crew. The airship, *Spirit of America,* was supposed to circle around before landing after videotaping an NBA game at the Staples Center in Los Angeles, but it came loose from its moorings, bumped into a parked truck, and then crash landed into a fertilizer pile beside a plant nursery. The cameraman suffered a knee injury from the December 2003 accident and was taken to a hospital.

Crazy Like a Fox

In the 2000 presidential election, Pat Buchanan's Reform
Party running mate, Ezola Foster, a longtime opponent
of most government social programs, admitted in August
2000 that in order to get California workers' compensation
benefits, she submitted a false document in 1996. Foster
claimed to have had a "mental illness" that entitled her to
draw money for a year before her retirement as a typing
teacher in 1997. When the issue of her mental stability
came up during the campaign, Foster claimed her "mental
illness" was worked out "between my doctor and my
attorney. It's whatever the doctor said that, after working
with my attorney, was best to help me." Foster founded
Black Americans for Family Values and wrote the book
What's Right for All Americans.

Carrying a Torch

According to an October 31, 2000, article in the *Inland Valley Daily Bulletin,* a twenty-nine-year-old man accidentally drove over a cliff in a recreation area in Ventura County. Police reports indicated that the cause of the accident was that the headlights on the unidentified man's off-road vehicle had failed and he was using a flashlight instead.

A Flash in the Pan

Bob Manion was denied permission to perform as his loveable alter ego, "Flasher the Clown," at Clayton's Walnut Festival in January 2001. Organizers began worrying about "Flasher's" appropriateness, according to a February 11, 2001, article in the *Contra Costa Times*. His act consists of him carrying a small Yorkshire terrier inside his pants, which he reveals by flashing open his coat (he also encourages the children to pet the puppy).

A man who was suspected of burglarizing a Beverly Hills home was frantically running away from police. He turned to see how much distance there was between him and the officers and slammed into a low-hanging tree branch, knocking himself unconscious.

Ham Fisted

A Ralphs supermarket in Livermore offered a free ham to anyone buying $50 or more of groceries. But when Rachael Cheroti saw her total ring up to only $48, she threw a fit and demanded the ham anyway. According to police reports cited in the April 11, 2001, edition of the *San Francisco Chronicle,* the manager acquiesced and gave her the ham. But Cheroti wasn't satisfied and demanded more hams on the premise that she spent so much money at the store every month, she deserved them. The manager rebuffed her assertion and refused to hand over any more hams. Cheroti then rammed the manager with her shopping cart, pinned him against a wall, and wrestled him to the ground. When police arrived, she ham-handedly wrestled one officer to the ground, as well, but was eventually arrested.

Strip and Rip

When a customer at the Dream Girls Cabaret in San Diego told stripper Lawanda Dixon that he didn't want a lap dance, she cut him—not with a snide remark but with a knife. "He (Melik Jordan) said no," San Diego police Det. Gary Hassen told Reuters on September 1, 2005. "She pulled a knife out of her bag and stabbed him." Even though police never found out why a topless dancer was carrying a bag, Dixon was arrested for assault with a deadly weapon and possession of methamphetamine.

A Tangled Web

Blobs of white material up to twenty feet in length descended over the San Francisco Bay Area on October 11, 1977. Pilots in San Jose encountered them as high as four thousand feet. Migrating spiders were blamed, although no spiders were recovered.

All's Well That Ends Well

During World War II, California, Oregon, and Washington were all attacked by the Japanese. On February 23, 1942, thirteen shells fired from a Japanese submarine hit the Bankline Oil Refinery at Glorieta in Southern California, causing damage to one oil well.

In Pacific Grove, according to City Ordinance No. 352, it is a misdemeanor to kill or threaten a butterfly.

A Bunch of Bunk

In March 1967, Max Scherr, the founder and editor of the alternative newspaper the *Berkeley Barb,* ran a satirical story in the hopes that he could dupe the authorities into outlawing bananas. In the story he claimed that dried banana skins contained "bananadine" a (fictional) psychotropic substance that could induce in the user an opiumlike euphoria. Even though the story was a joke, the national news media treated it like a real story and for some reason the "mellow yellow" banana buzz is still believed by many people today.

Not Child's Play

"It's really about the mind games," said Doug Walker, copresident of the Toronto-based World Rock Scissors Paper Society, which sponsors an annual contest. "There's a lot of trash talking and mental intimidation," he said of the 2003 contest, held at Roshambo Winery in Healdsburg, north of San Francisco. Approximately 120 contestants pounded their fists in hopes of walking away with the $1,000 first-place prize, according to a March 16, 2003, article in the *San Francisco Chronicle*. In the end, a twenty-year-old student from Oakland, Ana Martinez, used "rock" to smash her opponent's "scissors."

Flying by the Seat of His Pants

According to a December 19, 2002, article from Reuters, when customs officials at the Los Angeles Airport opened Robert Cusack's suitcase and a bird of paradise flew out, they asked him if he had anything else to declare. The Californian, who was returning from Thailand, responded, "Yes, I've got monkeys in my pants." Cusack was sentenced to fifty-seven days in jail for attempting to smuggle four exotic birds, fifty threatened species of orchids, and two pygmy monkeys into the United States.